BUYING USED GUITARS

Gerry Hayes

Published in 2021 by
Crooked Nails Publishing
Dublin, Ireland

Enquiries: gerry@hazeguitars.com

ISBN: 978-1-9196494-1-2

CONTENTS

INTRODUCTION

Heading to a music store and walking out with a shiny new guitar or bass is a relatively straightforward job. Granted, you've got to find the right guitar for you but, for the most part, there's not a lot of uncertainty about the process. Even a used guitar that's still mostly new, and maybe hasn't been played much, probably doesn't warrant much in the way of additional advice.

Dig just a little deeper into the used-guitar market, though, and you'll encounter older and more well-played instruments. Many will be in fantastic shape but, often, you might find a guitar with a snag or two. Being aware of some potential issues before you get too far in your guitar quest might lead to less stress (and possibly less expense).

What follows is a high-level round-up of the sorts of issues I'm often asked about *after* a player has made a purchase. This is not meant to cover every problem, or to go into a lot of depth, but it should give you an appreciation of some common things to look out for.

Much of this advice is universal but I'm going to try to separate it somewhat into tips for electric instruments and for acoustic instruments. Oh, and when you read 'guitar', you can probably substitute 'guitar or bass' most of the time.

MOSTLY ELECTRIC GUITARS

The basic checks are really those you can more easily see, measure, and inspect. And you absolutely should see, measure, and inspect them. Let's get started.

Action

Check the action is in a decent place. Of course, you can always set up the guitar to your own preferences later but, what you're looking for is the relationship between the current action and the saddle height. If the saddles/bridge are already set very low on the body but the action isn't correspondingly low, it might be difficult to set up for a lower action later on.

You'll ideally want to have some downward travel left on the saddle or bridge height adjustment screws. If the saddles are bottomed out, but the guitar's action is still a little high for your liking, that's a reasonable warning sign that the neck angle might not be correct. Worst case scenario here is that a neck reset might be on the cards.

For bolt-on neck guitars, resetting the neck angle might be as straightforward as removing the neck and shimming it for some back angle. Glue-in necks, though, are likely push this repair pretty deep into expensive territory.

Saddle screws

Since we're here, let's stick with the saddles. Check how freely the height and intonation screws move. These can easily get seized up with corrosion and guitarist sweat so give them a good once-over.

If there is some gunk or corrosion, take an even closer look. Once they start to seize, careless adjustment attempts may well have left the screws with worn slots/hex-sockets. Very worn stuff may have to be replaced and, depending on vintage, that could impact originality.

Freeing up these screws may involve complete disassembly of the bridge and maybe some tricks like soaking in oil solutions. It's not the most expensive job in the world but it's annoying and you should be aware of it before you make a purchase.

Collapsing bridge

Tune-O-Matic bridges can sometimes buckle under string tension. Over time, they start to sag in the middle and collapse into a concave/bow shape. In the worst cases, the bridge casing can crack.

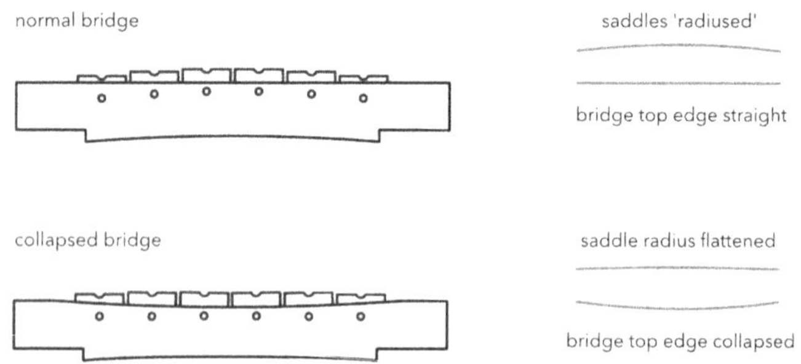

A bow in the bridge causes the saddle heights to change—those in the middle become lower—which can lead to problems getting a consistent action across the radius of the fingerboard. Collapsed bridges can sometimes be straightened but may need to be replaced.

Frets

Check fret condition. Push the strings aside and look for flattening on the fret tops or any wear spots. This wear will likely be most evident under the plain strings. It can occur anywhere (although it's location can give a fun indication of the previous owner's preferred styles and even keys).

Light fret wear may not be a problem, although you should play to make sure. As wear gets heavier, you may have to consider a fret level or—if the frets have worn too low—even a refret.

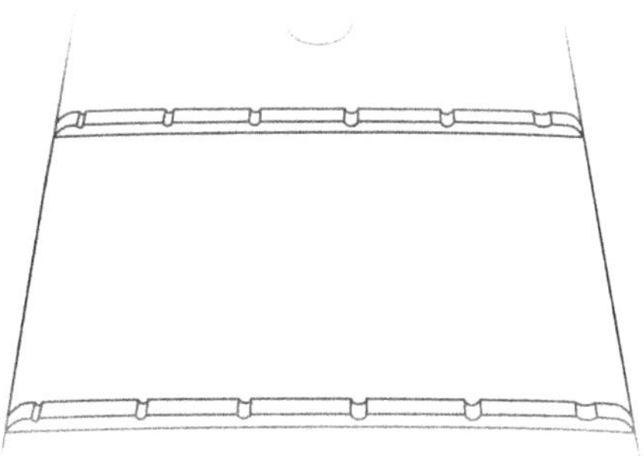

Uneven Frets

Play every note on every string. Do it carefully (but fairly—see note below) and listen for any intrusive buzzing. If there is, you may be looking at a fret level or some remedial work to get the frets in order.

The key word above is 'intrusive'. Guitars can buzz and rattle sometimes but don't sweat the minor stuff. If it's not killing a note or if it can't be heard through an amp, it may not be something to worry about.

Oh... Don't do that thing where you make it buzz on purpose. That'll just annoy the seller and they'll move you to the No Haggling category. Play the guitar like you play a guitar.

Fret ends

As a continuation of the above, look for any fret ends that seem high or that aren't pressed firmly down to the fingerboard. These may need the be glued down or replaced. Worst case, they may require a follow-up fret level.

Also on the fret ends, feel along the board for any roughness or sharpness that may be caused by the frets protruding past the edge of the fingerboard. Sharp frets will be annoying and you'll probably want to get them tidied up. It's not too big a job.

Bear in mind that loose frets, or those that poke out the sides of the neck, can sometimes be a symptom of a guitar that's become too dry. If humidity is an issue in your area (or the seller's), you might want to dig a little more deeply.

Fingerboard

Look for any divots or wear spots from playing. Most of the time, they're not a big deal but make sure you're ok with any that are present. If you're one of those players who like to grip pretty hard, divots under your fingers could lead to your pulling the strings sharper than usual while you play.

Check for any evidence of earlier refrets. Some wood is more 'chippy' and some refretters are less careful. Satisfy yourself with what you see.

Nut

Check the slots and make sure the strings are relatively snug. They shouldn't be loose or have any sideways travel.

Play each string open and listen for any buzz or rattle that might indicate a nut slot cut/worn too low.

You can perform a little rule-of-thumb nut height assessment but fretting a string at the third fret and checking for some space between the top of the first fret and the bottom of the string you're fretting. You should

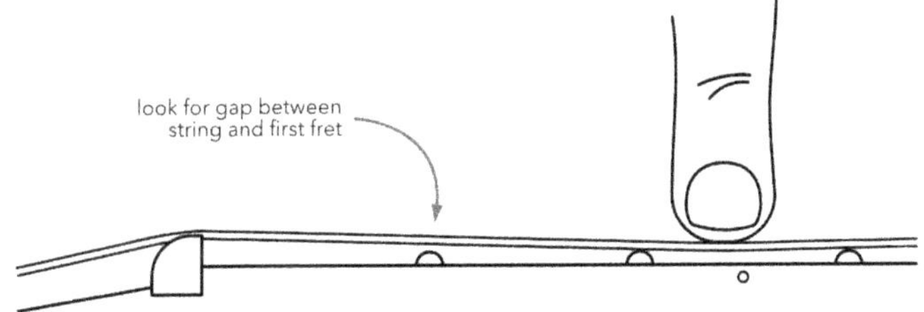

have a little bit of an air gap there. Repeat with all the strings.

Nut slots that are too high can easily be rectified but too low a slot will mean either a replacement nut or some work shimming the nut or back-filling the slots.

Relief

Following from the last point, now is a good time to mention relief. Excessive relief can be hiding a low nut slot or even some fret issues lower on the neck (more neck bow means more space for the string to vibrate and can disguise some problems).

To check relief, fret a string at the first fret and the 17th (on an electric) and assess the gap between the 8th fret and the bottom of the string. Too much and you might want to straighten the neck to make sure all is well.

How much relief is allowed for a given guitar depends on a number of things; player preference being high on the list. It's a little awkward to actually measure relief in a buying-a-guitar situation but try to get a feel for your own guitars before checking out prospective purchases.

Truss rod

And that brings me nicely to the truss rod. Whether you feel you can confidently measure or assess relief, you'll definitely want to make sure the truss rod is working so that you can adjust relief later.

Take a quick relief check as described above and adjust the truss rod nut to make sure it's working. Loosen and tighten the nut a little and check relief each time to make sure it's actually adjusting the neck.

Spend some time making sure that the truss rod adjustment nut or hex-socket isn't worn. this is really important. I see plenty of guitars with worn truss rod adjustments and, in some cases, it can turn into a relatively big job to put right. Adjustments, particularly hex-sockets can wear with time (although even more so with poorly carried out adjustments or the wrong tools).

Make sure the truss rod can be adjusted and that it has an effect on the neck relief.

Before we leave relief and truss rods, I should say a word about back-bow. It's the opposite of the neck relief we've talked about—the highest part of the bow is in the middle of the neck. Much of the time back-bow is present (which isn't often), it makes itself known by buzzing choking frets from the first to around the sixth or seventh. Instruments with dual-action truss rods can be adjusted to correct back bow. Standard, single-action truss rods can't address a neck that's back-bowed (although over-tightening a truss rod is, itself, sometimes the cause of back-bow—try loosening the truss rod to see if it comes good).

Tuners

While we're down at the headstock end, let's check out the tuners. Are all the buttons and screws present and correct? What about the bushings and mounting nuts?

You'd be surprised how often these parts can rattle loose and be lost. Press-fit bushings in particular can very easily go missing over time.

Check tuner operation. Ensure they work well and smoothly. If they're stiff or jerky, they'll need work or (probably) replacements.

Strap buttons

Check they're secure. Can you rotate them with your fingers? Repair is straightforward but it's good to know about before the guitar falls from your strap some day.

ELECTRICS

Pickups

Do the pickups work in all positions? Check each switch position to ensure the correct pickups (or coils, as appropriate for split humbuckers) are active. It's not always easy to tell from just strumming the strings so tap a screwdriver, or even a coin, off a pickup pole piece/screw to see if it's definitely active. You'll hear a clunk from the amp as the screwdriver contacts the pole. It's a good way to be sure.

Switch

Switch back and forth between all positions a few times and listen for any crackles or signal drop-outs. Noisy switches can be cleaned but may ultimately need to be replaced.

Pots

Rotate each pot all the way down and back up a few times. Make sure they're working as they should—volume adjusts the volume and the tone affects the tone.

Also listen for pops or crackles there too. Again, you might be able to clean them or you may have the install new pots.

Jack

Same story. Give the guitar-lead jack plug a bit of a wiggle at the guitar's output jack. Listen for any crackling or signal loss. Cleaning might help if there's a problem but a replacement is a much better idea.

STRUCTURAL

Breaks or cracks

Look for anything that will need to be addressed. Cracks, for instance will generally need to be repaired or they may get worse. Check all over the instrument but pay closer attention to areas that would have seen glue joints when the guitar was built: Centre-seams, headstock-ears, top-to-body joints, neck-fingerboard joints and, of course...

Neck joint

This is one of the most important joints on the guitar and you want it to be sound. For a glue-in neck, examine carefully for any cracks or separation.

Thin cracks in the finish, that follow the joint seams, are probably not a problem (although they bear watching over time, just in case). Any gaps or separation, however, is a sign that there may be a bigger issue. It doesn't take a lot of separation to alter the neck angle and make a guitar difficult to play. This is usually more of an issue for archtop-type instruments than solid-body guitars but it's not unheard of there too.

For a sound repair of a loose neck joint, it's likely the neck will need to be removed first and that's probably going to cost you. For this reason, you definitely want to check around the neck joint before handing over money to buy a guitar.

When we're talking about bolt-on necks, it's not unusual to find thin cracks in the finish, spreading from the corners of the neck pocket. These are almost certainly not structural and are typically only a concern if the aesthetics bother you.

Do, however, check that the neck bolts all tighten fully. Sometimes worn threads in the neck screw-holes can prevent the bolts from screwing all the way home. Try to tighten each, and make sure it snugs up fully. If it just keeps turning, it points to a repair in the future. Nothing major, but something that should absolutely be addressed.

Previous repairs

You'll want to look for any evidence of previously repaired breaks, dings, or cracks. Headstock breaks will likely be the one that will be top of list. If the repair is good, however, you probably don't have to worry about soundness. A well-repaired headstock won't be any weaker than the original (and there's even an argument to say it may be stronger).

Same applies to almost any well-executed repair. The glue is stronger than the wood itself and, providing it's done properly a repair probably isn't a problem from a structural perspective.

Of course, the aesthetics of a repair may not always be to your taste but that's an argument between you and the seller.

How to tell if a repair has been carried out well is difficult to advise on. I'd say that, many times, you can tell a repairer's pride in the neatness of a repair. This is a broad, sweeping generalisation that definitely doesn't always hold but, as a rule of thumb, it'll do. If a repair seems to be a mess of glue, patches, and poor finish touch-up, it might not bode well for its soundness. Sorry to give you such a crude yardstick as this but, barring a proper assessment of the repair from a (known) good repairer, that's mostly what you have to go on.

One tip I can give is to look to the gaps and alignment. If any glued repair seems to have wide glue joints, that might be an indication of a problem. Good clamping is key to sound repairs and, if the joint hasn’t been well clamped, the glue won’t adhere so well. Tight, closely fitting glue-lines are typically a better sign than wider gaps. There are, of course, exceptions but it’s a good rule of thumb.

Check the alignment of repairs too. Does everything line up and run the way it should? Has anything been misaligned during a repair glue-up procedure? Look for lips and edges around repaired areas. Run your fingers over any glue joints—they'll often be able to recognise some misalignment if it's there.

FINISH AND AESTHETICS

And that seems a good place to move on to talk about how things look. Finish touch-ups, or even refinished instruments, are obviously a big concern for many buyers. This is multiplied when you're shopping for a vintage instrument. The extent to which these sorts of things affect your decision—and your negotiations—will depend on a lot of things, not least of which is how well any repair or refinish has been executed. If the work is well done, you shouldn't have any issues beyond originality. Of course, originality impacts value so this gets complicated.

Best advice I can offer here is to do some homework to get an appreciation of how this work can impact value in the instrument you're considering.

Finish chips, dings, cracks, etc.

If you're buying an older instrument, you're probably ok with a certain amount of playing wear. I sometimes speak with customers who have bought older guitars and want to have them touched-up to hide any previous wear marks. Of course, that's perfectly valid if you feel strongly enough but bear in mind you could end up paying more than you bargained for once you add in repair and refinish costs. Possibly more important, you may actually devalue some instruments by making them all nice and shiny again.

I'd advise you to have a think about where your threshold for wear lies. If you're the type who loves a flawless, pristine guitar, maybe the second-hand market shouldn't be your first call.

Stand damage

Before we get off the subject of finishes, we should talk about stand damage. Some guitar finishes react poorly with the materials used in some guitars stands and hangers (and even straps). Finishes like nitrocellulose can bubble and scar after prolonged contact—it's not pretty.

Many modern accessories are 'finish-friendly' but some aren't, and it certainly wasn't the case in the past. The locations of this damage are not always in places we examine often so it's easy to miss unless you go looking.

Check around the headstock, where it widens (the area a hanger would grip). Check the bottom edge, either side of the strap button (where it would rest on a stand). Check around the strap buttons themselves in case a reactive strap material was used. The back of the neck, where it might rest against a neck holder on a stand, will probably be more obvious but don't forget.

Oh, and it's not exactly common, but I once saw this sort of bubbling finish reaction all around the edges of a nice instrument that had been stored in a very cheap case. The case had obviously been lined with something that was far from finish-safe. That's probably not something you'll encounter; I'm mentioning it to emphasise the damage that can occur from this sort of thing.

Binding

Check all the binding. All of it. Especially on older instruments. You're looking for any separation or shrinkage. Some bindings can shrink over time and you may find some gaps where one piece of binding butts or mitres against another. On the body, check places where binding might be joined (like at the centre-seam by the end-pin) or might end (like where the body meets the neck). On the neck, look to the corners (where the sides of the fingerboard meet the end or the corners of the headstock) and also the nut end of the fingerboard edges. You're looking for gaps where the binding has shrunk back along its length.

Also look to the 'interior' curves on the body. Binding shrinkage at the waist area can pull the binding from the body and leave a gap between the two.

Given the right (or wrong) conditions, older celluloid binding can actually 'rot' over the years. This can leave you with binding that pitted, bubbled, or warped. It's not pretty and it can be costly to properly repair or replace.

Oh, and check fingerboard inlays (or any other inlays) just as you would the binding. Check for shrinking, looseness, warping, etc.

Most of this binding stuff will be of more concern with an older guitar but, as old/vintage generally means more money, you'll want to be thorough.

Pickguards and other plastics

Following on from the binding, much of what was stated there applies also to the other plastic parts. Depending on material or vintage, you can find all the same sorts of shrinkage, warpage, and even rotting/disintegration mentioned above.

Check around the screw holes. You'll frequently find small cracks that occurred as the plastic shrank but the screw stayed put. Actually, this one is so frequent that you can almost disregard it as a 'problem'. These days, it's not unusual for relic pickguards and parts to include cracks at the holes. It's one of those things that's just a part of the vintage landscape. That said, it's something you should be aware of and you have to factor everything into your buying decision. These things may be more concerning in a more modern used instrument.

Hardware condition

We touched on this when we spoke about bridge and saddle screws. Of course, you can expect some wear on a used instrument but do assess the condition of all the hardware, particularly metal parts. Check the plating and determine if you're happy or whether you need to factor in cleaning or replacement parts.

GENERAL CLEANLINESS

Yeah, I know. It's a used instrument and you shouldn't expect it to be pristine. However, do cast a critical eye over it's general condition to satisfy yourself you can either live with it or can clean it.

For instance, guitars from homes/studios where people smoke a lot can become coated in a pretty thick and nasty residue. If you're a non-smoker, living with this might not be something you appreciate and it's incredibly difficult to clean off. As a slight aside, I reckon a couple of hours spent trying to clean this nasty, tarry gunk off a guitar could be a great way to encourage smokers to cut down.

Summing up this cleaning thing, a little bit of 'relic-type' dirt is probably ok but it's a good idea to consider where your cut-off lies before your heart overrules your head and you end up with a guitar you don't like playing. If you're someone that likes their guitars immaculate, you really need to think about how much you'll be bothered by someone else's dirt and dings.

MOSTLY ACOUSTIC GUITARS

It seemed to make sense to split up the tips for electric and acoustic instruments. While there's good stuff in both sections, if you're buying a used electric guitar, you can probably skip this section.

However, if you're buying a used acoustic instrument, you have more to think and worry about. There's an overlap here and you'll probably find it useful to read the electric guitar tips.

That said, I'll do a really quick round-up of those points. It's not a cut-and-paste—just a recap so check back if you need any more detail.

Also, a couple of the points already discussed in the Mostly Electric section have a very particular relevance to acoustic buyers so I'll expand those.

THE BUYING-TIP ROUND-UP

Make sure the truss rod works and its adjustment nut or socket isn't worn (see below for more on relief). Check the nut slots are not to wide or too low. Check the tuners work smoothly and that all their parts are present and correct (press-in bushings go missing quite easily).

Check fret condition and determine if a fret level or refret might be called for. Look for loose fret ends or any that protrude past the edge of the neck.

REPEATING MYSELF

Here's the part where I repeat myself somewhat. As I mentioned, some of the stuff already discussed is even more important for acoustic buyers. I want to expand a little on these so they don't bite you in the butt.

Action and saddle height

Even more relevant here than on the electric side. Obviously, with a fixed-height saddle, action adjustment isn't so straightforward but that's not the main concern right now.

Check how much height is left in the saddle and gauge that against the current action. If you feel the action could do with coming down a little but there's not much saddle height left, that could mean there's a neck reset in the guitar's future.

While some bolt-on neck guitars are a little more straightforward to reset, guitar neck resets are typically an expensive repair. That makes this particular assessment a real biggie for anyone buying an acoustic.

As a quick visual check, you can sight along the top of the fingerboard. The line/plane that runs along the top of the frets should look like it meets with the top of the wooden

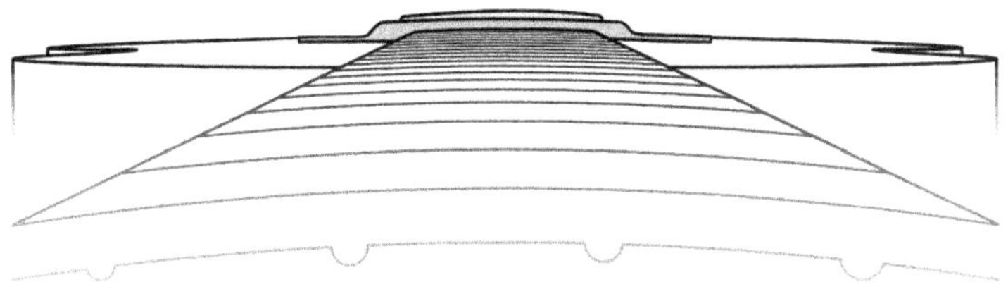

bridge. The image above shows a guitar with a neck angle that's very slightly underset. This sighting test is a rule-of-thumb check only but it will give you a good idea.

Even better (and a wise move if you're about to shell out a heap of money for a guitar) is to bring a long straight-edge with you. Rest it on the tops of the frets and see where the end contacts the bridge. In an absolutely ideal guitar, it will contact exactly at the top of the bridge. As the contact point moves lower down the bridge, we get deeper into neck reset country.

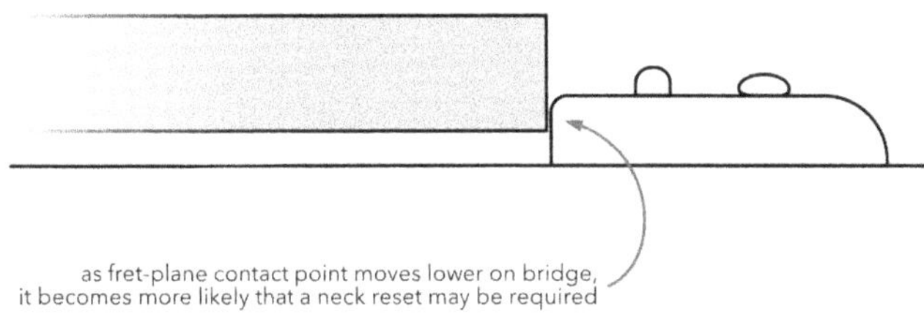

A guitar neck and body is under a lot of strain and, over time, the top and sides can pull and deform a little, and the neck block can shift so the neck angle changes. The first time many guitarists find out about the neck reset issue is when they try to address too-high action and find there's only a tiny sliver of saddle poking out of the bridge. What's probably happened is the saddle has been successively lowered over the years to compensate for the changing neck angle and now there's nowhere left to go. Nowhere except a (probably expensive) neck reset.

So, keep this one top of mind. Check the saddle height, check the action, and check where that plane along the top of the frets hits the saddle. Now, if you find there is plenty of saddle height left, you might not need to sweat a (slightly) low contact point too much. If the saddle's low, though... Time to take more care.

Neck joint separation

Do a quick check around the neck-to-body joint and make sure all the seams are tight. Some hairline finish cracks don't necessarily indicate a problem but look for any gaps. A thin feeler gauge can probe any separation you might find to see if its deep enough to warrant concern (a piece of paper like a nice crisp banknote will substitute for a feeler gauge in a pinch).

If you find any gaps, it's probably worth slackening off the strings a little to see if there's any movement in the neck joint. See if you can shift it when string tension is removed. That will probably mean a repairer has to remove the neck, assess and fix stuff, and re-glue the joint.

Neck relief

If the guitar doesn't have an adjustable truss rod, it's especially important to check whether neck relief is in a manageable place (not too much or too little). If the guitar has too much bow, it may require a decent amount of work to properly correct.

Back-bowed necks (where highest part of the bow is in the middle of the neck) are much less common. Newer instruments with dual-action truss rods can correct for back-bow but a single-action rod (probably the majority of acoustics) or no adjustable truss rod at all will require some repair work to put it right.

To check neck relief on an acoustic, fret a string at the first fret and at the fret just past where the neck meets the body (the 13th or 15th as appropriate). Assess the gap between the bottom of that string and the 6th or 7th fret. In the absence of a set of feeler gauges, your best bet is to try this with an instrument that's set up to your preference before leaving home. Get a feel for it that way.

Finish

In many circumstances, it can actually be more difficult to sympathetically repair finish on a well-used acoustic guitar. And—if it's even possible—acoustic buyers are probably even more keen on finish-originality than their electric buying pals.

Take a good look at the finish all over, including any touch-ups that may be present, and satisfy yourself with what you see.

Binding and pickguards

Plastics shrinkage can be problematic on acoustic guitars too. Look for the same issues around binding gaps and looseness. Pay particularly close attention around older instruments' pickguards. Because they're glued to the guitar top, if they shrink back, they can pull the wood with them, causing the soundboard to split or crack.

OTHER ACOUSTIC ISSUES

Bridge

Check for gaps around the bridge. Is it properly secured to the body all around? Bridges can lift and even pull off the soundboard so pay attention here. That crisp banknote feeler gauge will help here too. Probe any slight gaps between bridge and body (they'll tend to start at the rear of the bridge) and see how far you can insert the note. Anything more than a couple of millimetres (say 6/64") or so certainly bears watching. If it's confined to a very localised point, it might be nothing but it could be a sign the bridge is stating to lift.

Take a look out at the corners of the bridge 'wing' too. Often, as the soundboard shape changes under string tension, these areas of the bridge can be the first to come away. More in a sec...

Lastly on the bridge lifting issues, because it's a common problem, it's also a common repair. To be done properly, the bridge should be removed (carefully and properly) from the body before being re-glued. It's, unfortunately, not unusual to find this repair badly executed. Check the bridge is where it should be (look around it for any 'tan' lines or witness lines in the finish that might indicate the bridge has been reinstalled in the wrong position). Check also for excessive finish chipping or damage around the area. Too much glue, and wide glue-joints, are a bad sign too.

Intonation

Because you can't just turn a screw to adjust intonation on an acoustic guitar, it's worth checking that you're in the ball park. Absolutely perfect intonation across all strings and all frets isn't the aim here. That's not really possible on any fretted instrument and an acoustic saddle means there will, almost certainly, be some compromises.

However, even if the bridge hasn't been removed and replaced as noted above, it's not unheard of for an acoustic (particularly older instruments) to have it's bridge and saddle slightly 'off' where they should be. Fixing this can be relatively involved so do a quick intonation check to satisfy yourself that it's ok for you.

A quick aside on this: Intonation is the result of a lot of variables so bear in mind that a good setup of an instrument can go a long way towards rectifying some minor issues here. It's not going to address a misplaced bridge but, if the guitar is currently not set up terribly well, it'll probably help.

Soundboard

Despite being referred to as 'flat-tops', the majority of acoustic guitars have a slightly domed soundboard. It's higher in the middle—around the bridge—and it gently arcs down to the sides.

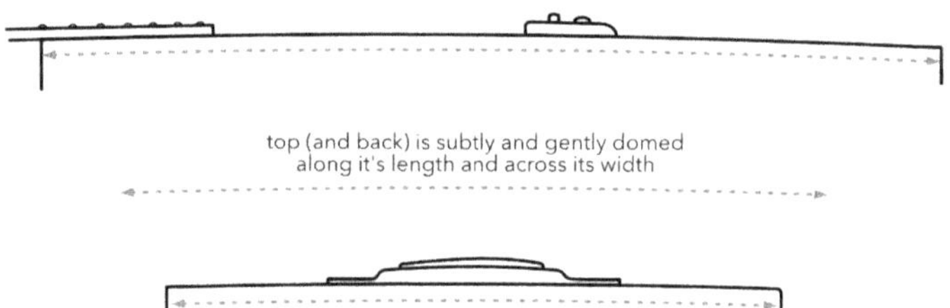

However, it's not a terribly high dome, and that 'gentle arc' thing is important. Too high a dome could indicate a problem, as could the presence of any buckles or wrinkles in the top.

Following on from the bridge-related tip above, the area around the bridge—and any lifting of the bridge—can be a symptom of a top that's deforming or doming too much. As the soundboard domes more in the middle under string tension, the bridge stays more or less flat so it starts to separate. The bridge wings/corners, as mentioned, can be first to show separation.

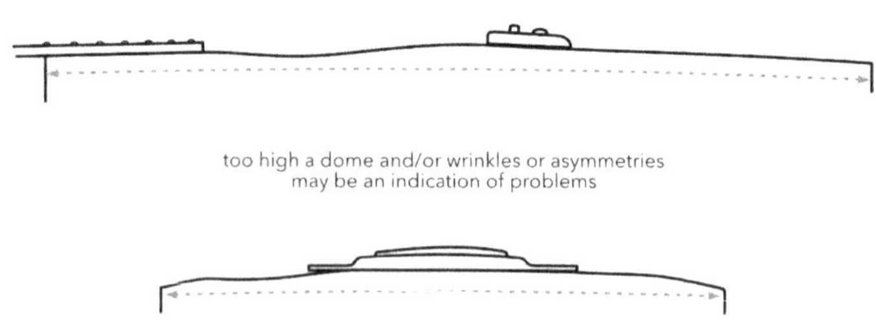

Look for any unevenness in the dome (a straight edge can help here but even a sheet of paper, folded over will work in a pinch. Uneven arcs may indicate a structural problem like weak or loose bracing underneath.

Check the soundboard for wrinkles or buckles. Around the sound-hole is a prime area to examine. A little deformation on an old instrument might not be a major worry but heavier buckling probably warrants caution.

We'll talk a little more about the soundboard when we consider humidity later.

CRACKS AND SEAM-SEPARATION

Examine along the centre seams on the top and back. Same goes for any other seams—a multi-piece back for instance. Check the joints where the top and back meet the sides. You're looking for any separation.

Barely open cracks are typically a minor repair. Larger cracks or big gaps may close up if properly humidified, but may need more work, especially if they've been present for a longer period.

Previous repairs

Well carried-out repairs of structural things—seam-separations, looks braces, and the like—are likely not a concern. In fact, some previous repairs can be considered a plus point.

A properly executed neck reset, for instance, will probably buy you some considerable longevity on many guitars. For most steel-string guitars, a neck reset becomes more and more of an inevitability over time. Having had someone else pay for it means you might have avoided a hefty repair bill.

Other things, like crack repairs, are also not a problem if they're done well. Of course, please satisfy yourself these things are well executed. Even if the seller tells you the neck has been reset, you should still check the saddle, action, and neck joint to make sure things look good.

INTERNALS

Oh, yeah! The serious acoustic buyer comes fully loaded for inspection. A small mirror and a flashlight are invaluable tools if you're about to spend a lot of money on an acoustic.

Slacken off the strings and shine your light in. You'll be able to get a good view of most of the back. Lay the guitar down and insert the mirror and then you'll be able to see what the underside of the soundboard is like too. It can sometimes be very revealing.

Bridge plate

Take a look at the bridge plate condition first. See how the string ball-ends sit on the plate. Ideally you want to see them snug against a clean, unmarred piece of wood. Of course, older instruments will have some wear but watch out for ball-ends that seem to have pulled deeply into the plate.

It can occasionally happen that a bridge plate will split, usually from hole to hole along its length.

Bridge plate repairs can end up being pretty expensive. Sometimes, wear can be patched up relatively non-invasively but, other times, the bridge plate will have to be replaced. That's a pain in the ass job that's difficult to do well—a good excuse to make sure it actually has been done well if the current owner tells you the plate was already replaced.

Braces

Loose braces will not usually be evident in a visual inspection with a mirror and flashlight. Sometimes they're not even evident after carefully probing with a feeler gauge. Now and then, you'll get lucky and see a loose brace end or similar but, unless you want to spend an hour up to your elbow through the sound-hole, you're really just looking for obvious issues here.

Check for braces that are clearly broken (it happens) or missing (also happens). Look for loose ends (often the first are to go and sometimes easier to spot). If you suspect a loose brace, you can try pushing on the area, from the outside, with your thumb. Sometimes, you'll hear a creak as things that shouldn't move, move.

Previous repairs again

Looking inside, you'll get some idea of how well previous repairs have been executed. It's hard to be neat, working blind with your arm through a sound-hole, so neatness is a good indication that someone has take care with their repair.

Cleats are small pieces of wood that act as 'ties' to help reinforce crack repairs. You may well see them if some repairs have been done. On a guitar's top or back cleats will, ideally, be thin and have a reasonably small footprint. They'll hopefully also be relatively few in number. This should avoid their having an impact on the guitar's tone.

Knowing all of this, look out for messy repairs. Lots of glue residue that hasn't been cleaned, or big hunks of material glued in to try patch cracks are probably signs of someone who could have taken more care.

It's worth my saying that poorly-executed repairs could harm an instrument's tone. A slab of plywood the size of a credit card that's been glued in to reinforce a crack probably isn't something you want to see. However, if you thought you liked the guitar's tone before you popped a mirror inside, maybe it's not a deal-breaker. It likely will, however, affect the value if you ever sell the guitar so it should affect your negotiations when you're buying.

ELECTRICS

If there's a piezo pickup installed, assess it for overall output and string-to-string balance. Check that the output jack isn't loose or crackly (give the jack plug a wiggle when plugged in).

Check all the knobs, switches and sliders on the preamp. See that the tuner works. Oh, and make sure the preamp and/or its bezel is secure in the guitar side (sometimes those little screw holes can strip and the screws can be lost).

CLEANLINESS

In addition to the notes on particular residues mentioned in the electric guitar tips, there's an added complication for acoustic buyers...

Smell

Probably because there's an open soundbox full of unfinished wood, acoustic guitars are much more prone to absorbing, and holding, odours from their environment.

Guitars that have been improperly stored can often retain a damp, musty smell that's pretty unpleasant. If you're a non-smoker, you might not like the aura of a previous owner's sixty-a-day habit. And, of course, if you play at church, you might raise a few eyebrows if there's a waft of the devil's lettuce when you open your guitar case.

I suppose that, over time (lots of time), these odours will eventually lessen or dissipate. That might take a while though and, since I'm unsure if Magic Tree air fresheners are guitar-safe, you might want to consider a smell test.

Humidity

Chances are, if you live somewhere that humidity is an issue, you're already familiar with what to look for. In too-dry conditions, the moisture content of the wood in your guitar will lessen. When it does, the wood will shrink.

This is most evident on the guitar soundboard. That slight dome we talked about earlier will begin to flatten out. This will take the bridge and saddle down with it and that will impact the guitar's action. If the action's super low and you feel things are more 'buzzy' than they should be, consider humidity. Try sighting down the neck. If the plane along the fret tops seems to pass above the top of the bridge, it may be the bridge has lowered as the soundboard flattened.

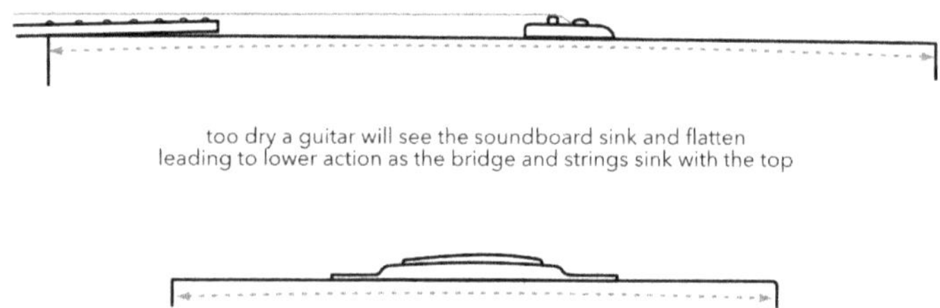

too dry a guitar will see the soundboard sink and flatten leading to lower action as the bridge and strings sink with the top

You can use that piece of folded paper as a straight-edge again. Place it across the guitar body just behind the bridge and get a feel for how flat or domed the top is.

Top and back cracks and seam-separations are a frequent symptom of a dry guitar too. Check for existing or repaired gaps.

You can also look to the frets. Fret-ends protruding past the sides of the fingerboard can be an indication of a guitar that's too dry. The fingerboard shrinks across its width and the fret ends poke out, ready to lacerate your fingers. Staying with the neck, it can bow more, meaning it might not be as straight as it would be if properly humidified.

Dry guitars can usually be brought back through re-humidifying them. This is often enough to close up any separations you might have found (and should be done before attempting a repair anyway).

On the other end of the spectrum, a guitar that's over-humidified has sort of the opposite of the issues noted above. Look for an overly swollen soundboard or back. In the worst cases, you'll find a swollen top/back with a weird wrinkle around the point they connect to the end-block (because the wood there is glued to the end-block and can't rise like the rest).

Watch out for higher action because the bridge has raised up as the soundboard bellied. You might also find the fingerboard extension has risen with the top, causing buzzing as you play nearer the octave. Too straight—or even back-bowed—necks, swollen fingerboards (wider than the rest of the neck) are symptoms that could point to a guitar that's over-humidified.

Guitars are very often too wet because of their owners attempts to keep them from being too dry. Every damn guitar magazine and website has articles outlining the dangers of a dry guitar, along with advice on how to humidify it. Guitarists take these at their word and humidify instruments that don't actually need it. Not everyone, everywhere, all the time, needs to humidify their guitar. Invest a couple of bucks in a cheap humidity gauge and take the guesswork out of this. End of rant.

Being slightly reductive, a guitar that's too wet is not quite so dangerous or damaging as one that's too dry. Well, at least not so quickly. Too wet a guitar can stress glue joints and distort tops or backs. It just tends to happen a bit more slowly and, hopefully, someone notices first.

Of course, there are extremes where that's no longer true—you'll probably need to carefully consider if that flood-damaged guitar is really the right one for you.

Humidity pretending to be something else

I should mention that, some of these humidity issues can be mistaken for other problems. For instance, too wet a guitar will probably have a high action. Sighting down it's neck will seem to indicate that a neck reset might be warranted (that line along the fret plane will contact below the top of the bridge). Carefully drying the guitar over a period in an environment of around 50% relative humidity can normalise the guitar and 'cure' this problem. No neck reset required.

The same concerns exist for some of the other problems mentioned above. For this reason, it's worth getting a feel for some of the other signs of humidity imbalance. Be careful about taking the season and environment into account when deciding if a particular problem is really that particular problem.

And, in an incredibly annoying, 'both-sides', manner I should also caution you to be careful not to mistake actual problems for humidity. You need to be sure that, when someone says, "Oh, it doesn't need a neck reset; it's just dry," that they're correct. Check for other signs of humidity before you make the call.

INTANGIBLES

This stuff is all less concrete and not so directly actionable. But, it's valid and might help someone.

Shop with your eyes

It's important. Really. It's important the guitar looks good. It doesn't have to be pristine (unless that's your thing) but be conscious of anything that might grab your attention. Everyone has their *Level Of Acceptable Imperfections* and, if your mind keeps returning to a particular flaw or feature, give it some serious thought.

Can you change your Level Of Acceptable Imperfections (LOAI) to live with this thing? If not, one of three things will happen:

1. You'll end up being slightly miffed every time you pick up the guitar and it'll ruin your enjoyment of it.

2. You'll end up talking with me about repairs and touch-ups that might not be necessary to someone whose LOAI is different to yours.

3. You'll end up selling the guitar pretty quickly and who knows if you'll make the same as you paid?

Really think hard about your LOAI. I know for sure that a lot of us allow our hearts to rule our heads on this one.

Continuing the 'shopping with your eyes' theme, does the guitar look cool? That might sound shallow but it's really not. Even if you intend that this guitar never leaves your home studio and will never be seen by anyone else, you still want it to make you feel good. It should look whatever way you define cool. It should make you happy. Don't underestimate this or feel you're being shallow. You're not.

Shop with your fingers

Does it feel good to hold? Does it balance on a strap in a way that feels ok to you? Does that sharp edge on the bridge make your hand feel a bit raw and can you live with it enough to build up a thick, protective callus.

Does it feel good to play? A good setup to your preferences might make all the difference. A poorly playing guitar might be transformed completely and, even one in decent shape can be made to feel much better once it's tailored more to you.

Do be as realistic and objective as you can when assessing the playability stuff. If there are fundamental issues, it may take more work than a setup but some judicious tweaks can really help make a guitar feel like yours.

Shop with your ears

Does it sound good to you? Does it make the sorts of noises you want to to make? Don't underestimate this. It's one thing to try out a guitar through someone else's rig but it might sound different when you plug it into your amp. Yes, that's an obvious thing to say but it's easy to forget when you're buying a guitar from Richie Rich and test-playing it through his Dumble amp, in his fantastic-sounding live room. If you're considering a big layout for a guitar, it can be worth checking whether you can bring along your own amp to get a good feel for the tone.

Other people's opinions

It's impossible to do any sort of research on guitars with tout wading through a morass of other people's opinions. Don't get me wrong: much of this will be useful but it's important to remember that those people are not *you*. They're other people who have other people's opinions. Do your best to keep your mind open.

Just 'cos *shredmeister1992* once played a pre-war Martin and thought it was overrated, doesn't necessarily mean anything other than that guitar wasn't *shredmeister1992*'s cup of tea. If *crustyoldgit1962* feels that the Jackson Rhoads is "pretty pointless for such a pointy guitar", it just means *crustyoldgit1962* doesn't like it.

I'm exaggerating (a little) and being a bit clichéd and facetious here but you get the point I'm making.

It's hard not to internalise a lot of the stuff we hear and read but, while accepted wisdom may be accepted, not all of it falls into the 'wise' category.

When you're buying with an eye towards repair or restoration, it can be even harder to get through the opinion arena unscathed. Same goes for trying to determine the value for a particular instrument, especially if it's been modified. Read and research as widely as possible.

REPAIRS AND MODIFICATIONS

While not inevitable, it's very possible—even very likely—that the guitar you're considering will have had some work over the years. Deciding the best way to deal with these alterations isn't always straightforward. Before you start buying guitars, it's worth some thought to consider and clarify your position on this subject.

Modifications and their impact on value

If you're shopping for a vintage instrument, you might be interested in having it as original as possible. It's not unusual for buyers to examine the solder joints in a vintage guitar to try determine if they've remained unmolested since the instrument left the factory. Less original means less value.

A fair seller will know that many types of work on a sought-after vintage guitar means they'll probably get less for it.

For less vintage pieces (the ones in reach of us normal people), modifications can be a little more complicated. Whether the fact that the Squier in front of you has been retrofitted with some posh pickups makes it worth more is difficult to say.

When someone is upgrading hardware, the advice I give them is not to expect the new value of the guitar to equal the original value plus the cost of the fancy pickups. It doesn't really work that way. That said, for the right guitar, with the right upgrade, maybe you'll be willing to meet the seller somewhere in the middle. Other mods, you'll have to weigh up on a case-by-case basis.

This leads me to modifications you might be considering after you purchase the guitar. If you think you like the instrument but reckon you can't live with it unless you change the pickups, don't forget to factor that extra cost into your budget. If you must have some modification, its cost has to be included in your mental arithmetic when you're purchasing.

Buying to repair

And that, in turn, brings us to the idea of buying something with an eye to repair. Say you find a particular instrument you're really GASing over but it needs a lot of work to get into any sort of playable state. That can be an amazing, bargain-blessing or an awful, sunk-cost curse.

It definitely *does* happen that an uncared-for guitar can be bought cheaply and, even after the costs of extensive repairs, can end up as a fantastic instrument for less than the price of a prime example.

But, of course, it can go the other way too. And probably does more often. It's easy to get caught up in the enthusiasm for that wonderful guitar and find yourself chasing that dream, throwing wads of cash as you go.

Anybody buying anything should be aware of the **sunk cost fallacy**. Seriously. This goes double for anyone buying something to restore.

In my simple, guitar-repairer-philosophy terms, this sunk cost thing refers to our tendency to keep putting money or effort into something just because we've already invested money or effort into it. We instinctively feel it would be wasteful not to spend a thousand bucks to fix a guitar because we've already spend two thousand bucks on that guitar. It doesn't matter that, at the end, the guitar won't actually be worth three thousand bucks—not spending the repair money would make us feel we'd wasted the initial outlay.

So, sorry to be a buzzkill on this but put your rational head on when you're going into a situation where you may be buying to repair or restore. Do your homework really well. You need to understand the value of different examples of the instrument, in different states of repair. And, you need to have a really good appreciation of what work is going to be involved. If you're thinking of spending big money on an instrument, consider booking some time for an assessment with a good repairer.

Future mods

It's crossed all of our minds from time to time. What if my current guitar becomes a highly sought-after vintage classic in the future? Will this minor modification I'm considering knock thousands off the value?

Uh... Iunno. Maybe. Who the heck knows if your particular guitar will be worth anything in fifty years? Maybe it will. Maybe it won't.

My feeling is that it's your guitar right now and you probably have the best idea about what makes it right for you. Sure, you could pop your Squier Affinity Strat in an environmentally sealed glass case and hope that, in 2070, it's worth enough to buy a Low-Orbit Hover House in order to avoid the robo-zombies. However, I'd say it's probably best to play and mod your guitars the way you like right now.

And (cue sacrilege alarm), the same goes for any guitar you buy. If you want to put EMGs in your pre-CBS Strat, go ahead. Once you've bought it, it's yours. Do whatever you want. I might not agree with you, and neither might most people, but it's not our guitar.

So, if you're considering any mods—be they innocuous stuff on a regular guitar or obscene desecrations on a priceless vintage instrument—go ahead. The one piece of advice I'd give you is to maybe pop as much as possible of the original hardware into a zip-loc bag and keep it somewhere safe. That way, if you ever sell on the instrument, you get bonus points/cash for being able to provide some originality to the new owner.

FAKES AND SCAMS

Oh, yeah. They're out there. Most people are pretty good but some are really not. Beware the fakers, scammers, and chancers.

Counterfeit guitars

I can't leave a guide on buying guitars without a word on fakes and counterfeit instruments. This is not going to be the definitive resource on how to identify a fake, partly because it would entail a book of its own and, even then, would be incomplete. Also, many contemporary fakes seem to have been getting closer and closer to the instruments they're counterfeiting (I suppose a certain amount of kudos is due for the fakers). This makes it hard to give a set of criteria to identify a fake—things might be different in a year. I've written stuff in the past with tips on spotting counterfeits, only to have many of those tips be addressed by the fakers (I don't fool myself they're waiting on my blog posts or anything—they're just getting better at this stuff).

Counterfeit instruments fall onto a weird spectrum, too. There are some instruments, usually built by small, boutique, builders with the intention of replicating some hard-to-source guitar (or qualities of that guitar). You could almost call them 'tribute guitars'. For instance, you might find a builder making Les Paul-type instruments to the specifications of a particular model or era. If that builder pops their own name on the headstock, it's all well and good (although Gibson might have something to say about it) but, if they put a Gibson logo on there, things get muddier from a buyer's point of view. It's easy to see how someone could be fooled into thinking it's something other than it is.

There are arguments that, because this instrument may be replicating something that would otherwise not be within reach of most players, it's more justifiable. There are also arguments that the quality of some of these instruments is higher than the guitars they're aping. Whatever your thoughts on this, I think that once someone might be misled (deliberately or accidentally), it becomes harder to defend.

More common examples in the fake arena are the (seemingly increasing) numbers of East-Asian-made guitars made to look like popular models from the big builders. These things are pretty insidious. Sure, you could make the argument that it's a cheap way for someone to buy into a particular brand (although, of course they're not doing that) but, again, the possibility of someone being fooled is the part that really causes me concern. If someone wants to dig around the net and—knowingly—buy a fake Fender, fine. I don't really agree with it, but they've made an informed choice. If someone later sells that guitar without mentioning that it's not a real Fender, that's pretty crappy.

And, of course, that brings me to the people who fall into the 'pretty crappy' category. Some people will happily sell a fake as the real thing. Some will go further and will actually fake stuff themselves to try make it look like something it's not. If you want to buy a Fender logo and stick it on your Squier, go ahead. I'd feel you were maybe a little insecure but, it's your guitar. Someone who then tries to sell their "Fender", though... Pretty crappy.

Scams

If you encounter a scammer, a lot of the time they'll just be—what we, in Ireland, call—a chancer. They're probably not some master criminal with a clandestine empire of dodgy businesses. More likely they're someone who's trying something dishonest in the hope of making a quick buck.

That doesn't mean you should be complacent. Watch for some obvious red-flags like online ads with only photos from the manufacturer's marketing materials rather than the actual guitar. Look out for poor quality photos, or too few photos (online, you want to be able to see everything).

In real life, beware of anyone who doesn't want you to inspect the instrument (or to inspect it too closely) but I'll add this consideration here: Remember that private sellers don't run music stores and are unlikely to want two dozen different guitarists at their house, kicking tires. Don't ask to inspect guitars unless you're pretty sure you're interested in buying—get as much info and photos as you can up-front and satisfy yourself before you ask to inspect.

Because this is the real world, and because people can be understandably nervous about giving out their address, it's not necessarily a red-flag to have someone ask to meet in a public place. That can be a little worrying if you're buying, though. If you're planning on spending a lot of money, try get some sort of proof of identity to be sure the seller is who they say and so there's some sort of trail should the worst happen. Most honest sellers will be cool with that. Discuss this before you meet and you'll be able to come to some mutually agreed arrangement.

Watch out for those who are really anxious for a quick sale. If it's gotta be now, it's probably bad news. Oh, yeah... Don't buy a guitar from someone who pulls up next to you in a van or someone who approaches you in a bar.

Stolen gear

Just don't. If you have any suspicions that something might be stolen, don't buy it. It sucks. I've known too many musicians have gear taken from them, never to see it again. Don't buy anything you suspect is stolen. Of course, sometimes you just don’t know but, sometimes... you have a feeling.

Trust your feelings. If doing that can blow up Death Stars, it can guide you away from receiving stolen goods. The fewer opportunities to sell stolen stuff, the fewer pissed off musicians staring at a cleaned-out rehearsal room.

Caveat emptor

Let the buyer beware. Some people are crappy. Do your research. If you're new to all of this, see if you can drag along a friend who knows a little more. If you're going to lay out a lot of cash, consider booking an assessment by someone who's an expert (and who has no skin in the game).

They say you can't fool an honest man. Not sure that's quite true but it's a good rule of thumb. If something seems too good to be true, be really, really careful.

THE LAST WORD

That's a terrible sentiment to go out on. I can't let the last word here be a warning about con-artists and an admonishment about not being dishonest. That's bloody awful. Positivity is what we need here.

The world is not a bad place, really. The guitar and bass world is mostly a brilliant place (except for those people who turn completely unrelated forum posts into a way to brag about their gear). Ha!

Buying and selling guitars and gear is a fantastic way for musicians to move on stuff that's not for them and to get their hands on stuff they've always wanted. The second-hand guitar market has thrived for ages and it's awesome.

Go! Find something great, something weird, something with holes where there shouldn't be holes. Buy flawless gems of guitars and buy guitars that smell like they've spent some time in a sunken pirate ship. Buy a 'beater' and learn all you can from it. Buy something stupidly expensive and figure out how to explain it to your partner.

Get yourself the guitar you've always wanted and enjoy it.

I hope this book helps along the way.

THANK YOU

I'm just a guy who spends most of his time in a dusty workshop, hammering nails into bits of guitar-shaped wood. I love to write this sort of stuff when I can and it means a lot that you checked this out. Thank you.

If you liked this, it would be a massive help if you could leave a review for me at Amazon or Goodreads. Honestly... You'd be amazed at how much difference it can make if you write a review.

I hope you've found this useful. Good luck finding your next guitar.

Thanks a lot,

Gerry

P.S. I also write a (mostly) weekly email newsletter with tips, tricks, and occasional opinion about all of this guitar setup and repair stuff. If you haven't already, you can sign up at:

hazeguitars.com/subscribe

You should subscribe. People say nice things about it.

ABOUT THE AUTHOR

Gerry Hayes runs Haze Guitars in Dublin, Ireland. He builds guitars (sometimes), repairs and modifies guitars (almost all of the time), and writes books about guitars (when he can find a free minute).

He's pretty nerdy and keen on helping players to understand as much as they want about maintaining their guitars. He's written a number of books on guitar maintenance, including the popular **Sketchy Setups** series of guitar and bass setup guides.

You can check them out at:

hazeguitars.com/books.

ACKNOWLEDGEMENTS

A couple of quick thank-yous on this one.

First of all, thanks to Owen who sends me a lot of 'learning material' to keep my hand in at repairing vintage instruments. He gets the good stuff (and sometimes the challenging stuff).

Secondly, thanks to Peter, without whom I'd probably be doing something different. I'm not sure I've ever said thanks so here it is. Thank you. Sorry it took so long.

www.ingramcontent.com/pod-product-compliance
Ingram Content Group UK Ltd.
Pitfield, Milton Keynes, MK11 3LW, UK
UKHW021051270726
13967UKWH00012B/204

9 781919 649412